The Invisible Remote

The Invisible Remote

How Parents Can Control And
Accelerate The Academic Performance
Of Their Kids And Make Them Understand
That They Are The First Priority For Parents

Vishweshwar Rau

White Falcon Publishing

www.whitefalconpublishing.com

The Invisible Remote
Vishweshwar Rau

www.whitefalconpublishing.com

ISBN - 978-93-88459-76-1

To
My Grandfather and Parents

TABLE OF CONTENTS

ACKNOWLEDGMENTS

I have to start by thanking my awesome wife, Swetha. From reading early drafts to giving me advice on the content edit, she was as important to this book getting done as I was. Thank you so much.

This book would not have been possible without Brendon Burchard, who has been constantly mentoring me throughout the completion of this book. I am especially indebted to Rajiv Talreja for letting me know how important it is for me to write this book.

Special thanks to my student Ruchitha who made me understand that the real purpose of a teacher is not only academics but an all-round development of a student.

I also thank all parents for entrusting me with the career of their kids, who gave me the wonderful experiences of my life as a teacher.

INTRODUCTION
THE PROBLEM

Hi, I am Vishweshwar Rau. I am writing this book to help your kids excel in their academics by getting great scores and be successful. This book will also make you (parent) understand how easy it is to help them get great scores in academics without sacrificing the essence of childhood.

I have a few questions regarding your kid. Has your kid ever had any of the following challenges in his/her academics?

1. The kid is working hard, but scoring less.
2. The kid is preparing for exams, day in and day out, but forgets all the stuff once he/she starts writing the examination.
3. Kids in your family and friends are scoring good marks but your kids are left behind.
4. Your kid cannot remember what they read.
5. You feel humiliated to share the score of your kid with your family and friends.

I also have a few questions for you as parents. Are you facing any of the below issues?

1. You feel you are unable to control your kids.
2. Your kids feel you are not that cool as a parent.
3. Do they listen to everyone except you?
4. Your kid feels you are pressuring them to get good grades.
5. You are unable to communicate to your kids that whatever you do, it's for their good.
6. You feel scary when they are out of your sight.
7. You don't feel good when you meet their friends.
8. You feel you cannot control the behavior of your kid in your absence?

9. Are you facing teenage issues of your kid?

10. Your kids are not in your control?

If your answer to any one of the above questions is yes, then let me tell you, my parents have been going through all these throughout my academics and teenage.

THE CHANGING WORLD

As per statistics, the global literacy rate for people aged 15 and above is 86.3%. (The figures might change by the time you read this book. You can always refer to the latest figures at https://en.wikipedia.org/wiki/List_of_countries_by_literacy_rate#List_of_UN_member_states)

It looks so great to see 86.3% of the world's population can read and write but, how many of them are really knowledgeable, employable, successful and leading a happy life?

Leave about the world, dear parent…

- Are you knowledgeable?
- Are you employable?
- Are you successful?
- Are you happy with what you are currently doing?

At any point in time, in your so-called employable and successful life, did you ever feel this is not the life you wanted?

You will get your answer in chapter 10.

THE NEW REALITY

All parents want their kids to flourish in academics and lead a successful life; as a teacher, I don't see anything wrong in it. Kids are our responsibility and it is the birthright of every child to be successful and lead a happy life.

As I said, there is nothing wrong in dreaming big for our kids; however, as parents, are you giving the best possible facilities for your kids to excel in academics and life?

When I ask this question to parents, everyone says 'yes we are providing the best facilities possible'. Here most of the parents get me wrong.

Why? You will get your answer in Chapter 3.

And by the way, if your teacher would have asked the same question to your parents while you were a student, the answer would be exactly the same, but do you agree?

MY STORY

As a kid, I never focused on academics. For me, academics was the last thing on my priority list.

But you know how parents are; they always wanted me to excel in my academics even after me scoring average in every examination.

The expectation came from the fact that I was being coached by the best Mathematics teacher of our times, my grandfather.

Even my parents provided me with the best of the facilities for me to excel in academics. The problem was, my parents just focused on the results and not the process.

By the way, I have a huge regard and respect for my parents, for the single reason that I am here because of them.

But I give credit to my teachers Mr. Ram, Mr. Suman, Mr. Murthy, and this one great man who taught me what I am good at - my grandfather who molded me to be a person who I am today. These people did not focus on the results, rather they identified the potential in me and focused on the process. In this process, I evolved to be successful both academically and in life and most importantly, I am happy.

In my career as a teacher, I have been applying the same methodologies and a few new ones I learned in my experience to bring the best out of my students not only in academics but also in life so that they are actually very happy and successful.

As a parent, you share the same goal, right?

Since the year 2000, I have been in this job of creating happiness in my students' and their parents' lives. The happiest moment for me as a teacher is when I meet any of my students and they share their success story with me and tell me how my methodologies helped them exceed their goals in academics and life.

I will share more stories in chapters to come.

IT'S POSSIBLE... EVERY KID CAN BE BOTH HAPPY AND EXCEL IN ACADEMICS

In my 19 years of career as a teacher and mentor, I have seen all my students excel in academics and happy in life. All my students give me a purpose for my life. Being an average student myself for most academics and accelerating myself to the top slot was only because of my teachers and mentors.

I have seen both sides of the coin; I know how it feels to be called an average student and also how society perceives a topper.

The journey from being an average student to a topper was not easy until I found my great teachers Mr. Ram, Mr. Suman, and Mr. Murthy, but they came very late into my life, till then I was struggling to perform and score good grades.

Your kids are young (in school or maybe in college), and as a parent, you have the chance to change their fate very early in their life.

After finding great teachers with a Midas touch, if my life could change for the best then I am 100% sure that you can change your kid's life too.

WHY READING THIS BOOK IS IMPORTANT FOR EVERY PARENT

By the time you complete reading this book, I am sure you will evolve to be a great parent to your kids.

Normally, when your kids' friends come home, your kids normally skip introducing you to their friends. If you are lucky enough, they will introduce you as 'my parents'.

Here, by introducing you to their friends they are just informing their friends you are their parents and better be watchful when they meet you somewhere else.

Now think about this…

If your kid introduces you as 'my lovely parents' or 'my strength', what impact that will have on your relationship with your kids.

My point is clear, just giving birth to kids and giving them all the facilities is not parenting.

Parenting is much more than that. They train us for every job we do in our life; however, we forget to be trained for being great parents.

CHAPTER 1

MOTHER, THE FIRST TEACHER

Why the majority of kids end up getting low grades and even if they manage to score good grades, why do they end up not being happy in their life?

- You ask them about the future plan, they end up showing a blank face.
- You inquire them about their friends, they become intolerant.

- You ask them to join you for a party, they make all the excuses in the world.
- Your kid does not share anything with you.

However, do you know there are kids on the planet who:

- are happy and score good grades.
- have 100% clarity on what their goal is.
- are happy to introduce parents to their friends.
- are more than happy to accompany their parents to a party.
- are happy to share everything with their parents without a second thought in their mind.

Now, are you thinking 'Ahha! Only lucky parents have the fortune of having such great kids?'

You are wrong; parents are not fortunate to have such great kids, these kids are fortunate to have great mothers.

For ages, we have believed kids are more attached to their mother than father, and it's a fact that no one can deny. However, in this changing economy where both mother and father are working to design a better future for their kids, parents are losing out on the current needs of their kids.

Here most of the parents get me wrong; they stand up and shout at me to tell me:

We are providing all they need to lead a happy life.

We are giving them the best facilities.

We are giving them all they ask for.

We are sending them to the best schools.

We are giving them…

We are giving them…

The list goes on and on and on… never-ending.

Here, I want to be very blunt, I am not writing this book to please anyone.

My question is - what about the emotional fulfillment your kids are looking for when they need you, especially the mother. For example:

When they want to share the reason for a fight they had with their best friend.

When they want to show you how they got hurt while they were playing.

When they want to show you the star their teacher gave them.

When they want you to be with them when they are feeling low.

When they want you to play with them.

When they want you to praise them…

Are you with them? Answer this question very sincerely.

If your answer is yes to all the above, your kids are fortunate to have a mother like you.

I am sure if I ask these questions to your kid they will put a cross on every question.

If you are a working mother, the good news is you can provide all the good things to your kids.

You can provide them with a good lifestyle, good food, good school, and good vacations, everything that you can buy with your money.

However the bad news is, in the process of providing them with good things, you are forgetting to provide them with the most precious human being God has ever created "The Mother".

The mother's job does not end being a mediator between their kids and the father.
The mother's job is not confined to cook that delicious food.
The mother's job is not about fulfilling kid's need.

The mother's job is much more than anyone has ever imagined:
The mother's job is to precast her kids into great human beings.
The mother's job is to make her kids strong.
The mother's job is to train her kids to handle success and failure with open hands.
The list is never-ending…

I am not saying working mothers are not good, however, even if you're working you cannot shy away from your core responsibility of being available to kids when they need you.

In my opinion, both father and mother's highest priority should be their children. But sorry to say this, in my career as a teacher I have seen a majority of parents giving second priority to their kids, first priority being their job.

Stop for a minute and think - if you are not able to give time to the kids whom you brought into this world, why the hell are you working so hard on your job; just to satisfy your ego?

Then you expect your kids to excel in academics and lead a successful life.

I have also seen mothers who sacrificed their high paying jobs just to be with their kids or got a job where they would get time to spend with their kids and be available when they need them even if it was a low paying job.

Who Wins, Who Loses?

With my experience of handling so my kids at my business "AVR Coaching", I observed that kids who were more inclined towards their mother and spent enough quality time with her were emotionally very strong and had less pressure of academics. They even scored well and were on the path of becoming great leaders.

What I figured out…

Majority of the mothers, irrespective of working or not, send their kids for tuitions to provide that extra edge in academics, and they feel their job is done. Now that we paid the fee in full, it's the job of the tuition teacher to see they get good grades.

As a teacher, we are great at making your kids understand the complicated mathematics problem with ease, but only for those who are regular to the class. As a mother, it's your responsibility to see that your kid is regular to classes.

I am emotionally very attached to my mother; she is my pillar of strength and my first teacher to educate me the fundamentals of business. My mother used to take special care in my academics and she would wake me up for my mathematics class to be taken by my grandfather, at around 4:30 AM to 6:30 AM every single day throughout the year (irrespective of the seasons).

I used to feel that they were taking a revenge on me for some unknown reason, for this torture started when I was in class 3 and continued till I was in

12th standard. I still remember how I would die to sleep in the early hours and would hate to leave my bed, but as said, I never had the luxury of sleeping till 6 AM.

I never understood why even after not scoring good grades my mother was hell-bent on waking me up at 4 AM. Actually, she was not focusing only on my academics but putting me to that commitment of getting up early.

It has been 30 years now that I have never slept till 6 AM.

As a mother, do you have that commitment to teach your kids to be committed even if it takes to push them out of their comfort zone and at the same time being emotionally attached to them?

If you are a father reading this book, don't be too happy that I have been saying everything only to mothers, and there is no involvement of fathers in their kids' academics. If you really think so, my next chapter is dedicated to all the fathers out there.

CHAPTER 2
FATHER COMES NEXT

This word excites me since I am a father myself. For ages fathers have been isolated in the upbringing of their kids, a mother would take all the responsibility of their kids' academics, upbringing, and everything related to kids.

Fathers are isolated from their responsibility of making their kids' future by summing up cash for that future. However, as a father, do you know it's much fun and adventurous to see your kids grow, know their likes and dislikes? But most fathers don't even know their kid's favorite color or food and they pose as the best father on this planet.

A father's job is not just about earning financial safety for the family; it's the responsibility of the father to see that his kids are capable enough to earn their individuality. For kids to be self-sufficient and independent, it's the sole responsibility of the father to train them in that direction.

For that, you need to spend quality time with your kids.

"Help them understand themselves."

"Help them understand their career goals."

"Help them understand their academics"

Most importantly...

"Help them understand their strength and weakness."

In my career of 8 years as a working professional in an IT Company, and 19 years as a teacher and an entrepreneur, I can proudly say the transformation in me as a person, as a teacher, and as an entrepreneur only came after I started spending time with my son Nipun.

My teaching business "AVR Coaching" was totally drowning with only two students as I was not able to sail on two boats at the same time. Nipun was only one year old then. I took the toughest decision of my life; I resigned my high paying corporate job in 2013 to fully concentrate on my teaching business. I didn't know how I would cover the monthly expenses of my family. But I did take the decision.

After resigning my job, what I knew was I had the whole time in the world to concentrate on my business and take it to new heights. However, success in business was not that easy, even after many marketing campaigns, I could do only 20 admissions for that academic year. But what came was a blessing in disguise! I had time at my disposal which I could control. I started spending time with my son Nipun.

Spending time with my one-year-old kid was the best thing that could happen to me in life. I have not only seen my kid grow but was actually participating and playing a major part in shaping his thought process along with my wife.

How many fathers have this great experience in participating in the growing years of their kids?

Why mothers should have all the fun, even fathers deserve too....

"See that first smile on their kid's face."

"See them take that first step."

"Help them in their school homework."

A father has every right to equally know their kids as mothers do. I found this to be the message from God to understand my kid first, before understating and shaping the future of my students. Spending time with my son provided me with so many insights into my business, for kids are huge compilations of experience.

Kids...

"Don't know what failure is."

"Don't stop trying if they fail once."

"Have a lot of perseverance than any adult on this planet."

"Know how to take the risk, for they don't know what a risk is."

That's the reason every kid is intelligent till the age of 6.

It's after that we, as parents, start teaching them all the wrong things like -

"Failure is the end of life."

"Stop them from trying new things."

"We teach to be far better than their cousins and peers."

"We discourage them even before they take any step."

"We start imposing our aspirations on to them."

"We, the parents are the number one culprits to teach our kids what FEAR is."

But, should I tell you one golden rule, instead of teaching them what to do and what not to, learn from them. I promise, the learning from your kid can help you get that long-awaited promotion in your job or that one deal that would take your business to the next level.

I was struggling in my tutoring business, for I was concentrating on providing the best possible teaching to all my students which I was accomplishing to a far extent and completing the syllabus to make my students exam-ready. So that their parents are happy and bring me more business through referrals.

As a teacher, I never thought of understanding my students, but once I started learning from my son, I understood the child physiology. I realized that all kids are the same; they have the same thought process. As parents, we don't understand them and for our failure to understand them we blame them. I started implementing them in my business, for I knew my students through the process and started teaching them the same way I did.

But the results were astonishing this time –
"My students were never absent to my classes."
"They started understanding the subject well this time."

"They performed 60% more efficiently in their exams than they did previously."

Most importantly, they were happy to learn from a teacher who understood their point of view.

All my students tell me that I understand their feelings better than their parents do.

This sounds a bit weird, but there is no rocket science to this, I am able to understand my students only because I understand my kid.

As a father, did you take time and pain to understand your kid?

"Did you ever think from the perspective of your kid?"

NO, right?!

To be successful in life you need to understand your kids first (if you are a parent). Everything else will automatically fall into place.

CHAPTER 3
TEACHERS PLAY A VERY IMPORTANT ROLE

"A teacher's career should be by choice,
not by chance."

Teachers are an integral part of any student's life; they are the people who can precast your kid into a genius. In my teaching career spanning 19 years, I observed that there are only three professions where you don't choose the profession but the profession chooses you. Do you want to know the professions?

Here you go…

1) Teachers

2) Doctors

3) Actors

I may be wrong, but it's my perspective which came with my experience, however, I am ready to change my perspective if someone gives me better options.

You cannot become a teacher, a doctor or an actor if someone wants you to be in that profession. The best of the teachers and the best of the facilities provided by your parents cannot make you the best teacher, the best doctor or the best actor. You need to have that DNA in you; if you want me to say it bluntly, you need to be born for that job. However, you need to be trained to be the best.

I listed 'Teachers' in the first place, as for being a great doctor or an actor you again need to be trained by a great teacher only.

In your lifetime, did you come across someone who became a doctor or an actor for the sake of making pocket money? No, right?! But you will find so many people choosing teaching jobs only for the sake of pocket money. This is because no one will dare to put that effort, invest time and money that goes in to become the best doctor or an actor.

As per a survey, the time it takes to become an expert doctor is three years to eight years. And to be good at acting, you need to practice your craft for hundreds of hours unless you are blessed to be a born actor or a craftsman.

And for both the professions you need to have that attitude and willingness to upgrade your skill.

However, if you are unemployed, no one will suggest you to become a doctor or an actor. But will suggest you to start taking tuitions to school kids or become a teacher in a local school until you get a high paying job, even if it means putting the career of those small kids at risk.

Let us assume, unfortunately, your kid falls ill. And you have two options:

1) Your locality has a self-proclaimed doctor who has never treated people in his/her lifetime.

2) You need to travel at least 10 miles to find an expert doctor.

What will you do?

Do you risk your kid's life by taking him/her to the so-called doctor in your locality or would you prefer the treatment from an expert doctor, even if it means traveling all the way 10 miles?

As a parent myself, I am sure you will go for option 2.

But when it comes to education, parents are interested only in teachers who can make kids sit for two to three hours making them do nothing or just making them complete their homework.

There are hundreds and thousands of people out there who have started there so-called tutoring business only to make pocket money or to be self-employed until they get a good job.

"I am sure you will find one in your apartment itself."

But parents choose them as teachers for their kids only for 2 reasons –

1) Those teachers are very cheap or low-priced compared to a professional.

2) They are in the same apartment or locality.

If you are a parent of this kind, then congratulations! Your kids will never need any enemy in their life to ruin them; for their biggest enemy brought them into this world.

Below are two cases for your understanding, as a parent you better understand.

Case 1: Assume this; if any parent has taken their kid to a wrong doctor, the worst thing that will happen to the kid is the kid will die, freeing the kid of all worldly miseries. Yes, as a parent I do agree that the parents suffer an unmeasurable sorrow that no one can fill, and a guilt for the rest of their life for their decision of choosing a wrong doctor.

Case 2: Assume this; if any parent has taken their kid to a doctor who is expert with a great track record and comes with huge experience. The worst that will happen is you will end up paying a hefty bill to the doctor; however, your kid is safe, fit, and fine. As a parent, are you under the guilt of paying that hefty bill or happy that your kid is fit and fine?

"You Are Happy and Thanking That Doctor for Giving Your Kid That Excellent Treatment."

But while choosing a teacher for your kid, you will go for Case 1 because you feel that for a school kid spending that hefty amount for a professional teacher is a waste of money.

This thinking is more dangerous for your kid's life than choosing a bad doctor, for a bad doctor will kill the kid once and for all, but a bad/wrong teacher can ruin your kid's fundamentals and their thought process due to which the kid will die daily for not performing up to their capability or efficiency.

"You as a parent, for sure will not want your kid to be in that position."

For me as a teacher, teaching is a more noble profession than a doctor. As teachers, we mold our students at AVR Coaching to be great human beings who are confident enough and future-ready to face and overcome the challenges not only in their academics but also in life.

A teacher's duty does not end merely by the completion of syllabus, it's the duty of the teachers to guide and mentor their students to the correct career path.

A teacher's vision should be both short-term and long-term. Short-term for identifying the areas where the student is strong and elevating that to boost their confidence and also identifying the areas where the student is weak so as to work with the student and the parents to overcome that drawback.

A long-term vision for a teacher is much more important; a teacher should continuously communicate with the students to identify their changing behavior, hand-hold them during the time when they feel demotivated and helpless.

A teacher's duty is much more than just being a teacher.

A teacher has to wear different hats in different situations.

A teacher has to be a friend to students.

A teacher has to be a torch when the students go blank during their decision making.

A teacher has to be a parent when the student needs them.

A gifted teacher can tell what's going in the minds of their students just by looking into their eyes.

A gifted teacher can tell if the students understood the concept or not.

A gifted teacher will clarify their student's doubts in subject and career 'n' number of times without questioning student's capability.

A great teacher will envision the same kind of success and happiness for their students that they expect for their own kids.

Most importantly, a great teacher will never ever insult their students. Instead, they will help their students to overcome the challenges.

Do you find these qualities in the tutor your kid is going to? If yes, then your kid is in safe hands.

But, if your answer is 'No', then find a teacher who is good at their job with the above qualities. Else, your kids are at a risk of losing their self-esteem, their confidence and more importantly, their individuality.

CHAPTER 4
THE ROLE OF
GRANDPARENTS

This topic is very close to my heart. If there is anyone I need to thank in this world other than my parents and teachers that would be my grandfather.

He was more than a grandfather to me, he was a mentor and a teacher; he is the person solely responsible for what I am today.

After parents and teachers, if anyone can play a major role in shaping your kids' future it is their grandparents! There is no debate around it. The immense experience they have in the way they look at life, the discipline they have maintained in their life is unmatchable; for the current generation of parents, it is unimaginable.

Any world class school, college or university cannot provide the quality of knowledge that kids can get from their grandparents. Grandparents are the encyclopedia to see life from a different perspective, which will help kids to see the problems in life as challenges or opportunities making them better human beings.

But given the current concept of nuclear families, getting knowledge from grandparents is a luxury of its kind, which every kid cannot afford for a different reason only known to parents.

As a parent, can you provide that kind of knowledge to your kids, which you have never experienced in your life? I would like to quote a famous English quote here, which we have been hearing from our childhood days.

"You Learn From Your Failures"

Yes, this is true, however, does your child have all the time in the world to experience all the failures by themselves to learn and reach success? Is it practically possible?

No, right? The only solution for this is "Grandparents."

It's not mandatory to fail for learning and reach success (Success Is Not A Destination, It's A Journey). Success comes to those who continuously invest time and money for learning new things and fail differently, learning a new lesson from that failure, not to those who fail for the same reason time and again, simply giving a nonsense excuse that they have learned from their experience, every time.

There are so many failures that could be completely avoided by proper guidance and learning.

When Grandparents share their life stories (experiences), your childhood stories with your kids, imagine the kind of knowledge kids are gaining in their life.

Do you agree that your parents have done so many wrong things in their life and lost so much? For no person in this world is perfect.

It can be anything…

For you to relate, here are a few examples:

"Believing a wrong person in the business."

"Believing that idiot relative who happens to be your family member who took over your parent's property."

"Taking that wrong decision in business, due to which your parents had to suffer a huge loss."

"How your parents realized late in their lives that family comes first, not the society."

"How they were uncomfortable taking a risk, due to lack of knowledge."

These are only a few examples; I can give you "n" number of examples of this kind.

As I said before, it's not mandatory that we need to learn from our failures, we can learn more from the failures of others.

What if your kid could avoid most of the mistakes and failures in their life just by sitting beside their grandparents and listening to their stories? You can never get a better option than this.

I have learned so much from my grandfather, and I make sure my son learns from his grandparents. There is no better way to reach success and to be happy in life. My grandfather taught me Mathematics and discipline in life, he taught me to have a meaningful life.

When my students give me credit for mastering Mathematics, that credit is not mine, it totally belongs to my grandfather. For he was the person who believed in me and taught me the nuances of mathematics which I, till date and till I am alive on this earth, will keep transferring to all my students so that they are happy and successful.

My grandfather gave me the gift of earning my bread and butter and an opportunity to change the lives of so many kids. However, it's not mandatory that every grandparent should teach their grandchildren mathematics for their success in life.

The knowledge I obtained from my grandfather, is immense, which is helping transform the lives of hundreds of my students for the better.

So, if any day you see your kid chatting for hours with their grandparents, do not yell at them and ask them to take out their school books and study.

Instead, thank God for providing your kid the opportunity to gain years of immense knowledge doing just nothing.

CHAPTER 5
HANDWRITING IS CRITICAL

"I saw that bad handwriting should be regarded as a sign of an imperfect education."

— **Mahatma Gandhi**

In the era of smartphones and laptops, parents have forgotten the importance of good handwriting. In my experience, I have seen that parents are concerned about their kids' handwriting when the kids are in their teens when changing a kid's handwriting would be next to impossible. The concern comes from the fear that their kid might lose score in examinations only due to their bad handwriting.

Yes, it's a fact that kids lose their score due to bad handwriting; I have seen my own students missing out that higher grade only due to bad handwriting. As parents we need to understand, a kid is not blessed with good or bad handwriting, it's the duty and responsibility of the parents to see that kids practice handwriting. Good handwriting is an art which cannot be mastered in a year or two; it has to become a habit, which can only form with years of practice.

Parents have to start working on kids' handwriting when the kids are five-years-old.

As a kid I remember, how my father used to strictly make me write three pages every day, which helped me improve my writing year after year. I didn't know good handwriting was so important for any person till I went to SSN Office in the United States.

People Appreciate Good Handwriting (I Thanked My Dad For The First Time)

When I landed in the United States for the first time, I had to apply for my SSN (Social Security Number) so I went to the local SSN office where the officer gave me a form to fill my details.

I filled up the form and gave it to her then and there, she checked my form once and called her other colleagues to her desk. I thought she was asking them to check my form, but I realized she was actually showing them my handwriting. Everyone there asked me how come I had such a good handwriting, with so much respect in their eyes. I proudly said it was because of my dad. For the first time, I felt, how great a visionary my dad is.

It really feels great when people from another country respect you for your handwriting, for they realize the hard work that goes into practice.

If my handwriting is good, it's only because of the care my father took for improving my handwriting.

CHAPTER 6
KEEP PRACTICING

"I hated every minute of training, but I said, 'Don't quit. Suffer now and live the rest of your life as a champion.'"

– Muhammad Ali

As a teacher I believe, no kid is weak or intelligent it's only about how we train them and motivate them to practice.

If there is one thing any person should be doing mandatorily, it is practicing their skill.

It's only the amount of practice which differentiates an expert from a mediocre.

I have seen parents who are overambitious about their kid's career and want them to excel in every competition they participate. It's so ridiculous to expect one kid to master all the skills. Most of these kids end up being "Jack Of All Trades, Master Of None."

Instead of forcing your kids to put their hands in everything and not succeeding in anything, try to find out the niche of your kid and make him/her master the art by getting them the best teacher possible who can polish their skill further.

School Academics are no exception for this; unfortunately, our education system is designed in such a way that only students who score good GPA (Grade Points) are considered to be intelligent, others are seen as failures.

Forget about society, even the parents consider GPA as a tool to gauge their kid's intelligence.

I agree primary education is absolutely necessary, but only education cannot decide how successful your kid will be. Who knows your kid might end up offering a job to one of his/her classmates who was a topper in their batch.

Practicing is the only way to master a subject or a skill.

The most important point to remember is practicing your skill, only under the person who is an expert in that field.

If you want to master "Mathematics", the only way to master is to get help from a teacher who is an expert in mathematics for school academics, not from an "English" language expert.

Most teachers and parents think practicing makes kids perfect, but it's only half the truth, the complete truth about practicing is – "Practicing the right way under a right person will make you perfect."

To master a skill or a subject, a kid has to avoid practicing in a single direction.

For example, if a kid has to master batting skills in the game of cricket, he has to practice with different kinds of bowlers; the kid cannot say to the opposite team, I am good at facing the fast bowlers, so make them bowl to me. It sounds so ridiculous.

So the next time you ask your kid to practice his/her mathematics problems, just don't ask them to do every problem 10 times or 20 times, that way your kid will only remember that single problem, and you cannot ask your kid's teacher to give him/her test only in that problem.

Instead, make them practice the concepts of that particular topic, give them practice problems, you can download so many problems from the internet, ask them to solve those problems, see if they applied all the formulas and implemented the concepts correctly. If they did, great, else sit with them and work out on the weak areas.

It not only applies to a subject like Mathematics but also goes well with all other subjects too.

Let me explain with an example of my own student. Her name is Aishwarya (Currently pursuing her degree in Medicine). She came to me for coaching when she was in class 10th.

For one full week, she was just attending my classes and going back. I was not sure if she was understanding the concepts or not.

After ten days, I conducted a test in mathematics. But she was absent, which was not new to me as a teacher; most students try their best to escape a test. The next day I asked her why she was absent; her answer was, "Not Feeling Well." (The most common answer to escape a test).

This continued for around 5 tests. In between, I called up her parents and enquired about her health; they told me, she was really not feeling well. And to my shock, they said that this was the case only when she had to attend a mathematics test.

I understood she had a phobia towards this subject.

The next day when she came to the class I had a one-to-one discussion with Aishwarya, about her fear of attending Mathematics tests.

It was during this discussion that I found out she was actually good at understanding mathematics but could not implement the knowledge she had. The problem of implementation came due to a couple of reasons.

1) Lack of professional guidance in her previous classes.
2) Her previous teachers showcasing Mathematics as a demon.
3) Lack of practice in the correct direction.
4) Lack of motivation.

After a discussion with me, the next day she came to me and said, "Sir, I want to be a doctor; it's my passion and the biggest goal of my life. However, to reach my goal I have to at least pass in Mathematics. Please help me score passing marks in the subject, I will for sure, become a great doctor." I still remember tears in her eyes when she was telling me about her passion for becoming a doctor and how Mathematics was becoming a speed breaker in reaching her goal.

From that day, I started working on changing her mindset towards mathematics. Her parents were more than happy to help me work on reprogramming her mind.

My only condition was she will never give an excuse and believe me, she never gave an excuse.

We chalked out a plan for her and made her practice different problems. I sat with her and told her where she was going wrong and why. Slowly, the number of mistakes she did in solving the problems started decreasing, with every practice session.

With this, she gained confidence in herself, and the fear of mathematics slowly vanished from her head. She ended up scoring 90% in mathematics. And now, she is happily pursuing her passion for becoming a doctor, oops!! A great doctor.

This was my experience; you can apply it to any subject and to any field, to get outstanding results and to boost your kid's confidence.

CHAPTER 7
CHOOSE FRIENDS WISELY

If I need to put a definition for a good friend, I would say, "A friend is a person who would laugh with you and not on you."

To be successful in life, it's very important to be in the company of only one good friend, rather than having a bunch of so-called friends.

Good friends are people who would criticize you to bring the best out of you. They scold you, they slap you, they fight with you, and they will go to any extent to stop you from doing anything that is wrong or unethical.

We cannot choose who our parents should be.

We cannot choose who our teachers should be.

We cannot choose the university to study; it depends on the score in your entrance examination.

Most of our life we do not have the luxury of choosing what we want.

Fortunately, the only relation that we can decide on our own is friendship. So make the best out of it.

Great friends are very hard to find, the world is full of opportunists who are always waiting to exploit you. So, how to find great friends? Keep the below points in mind before you start believing that you did find a great friend.

1) Good friends have great communication.
2) Good friends are not diplomatic. If they do not agree with any of your opinions, they will say it point blank.

3) Good friends are ready to ask your help when they need and they do not step back when you need help.
4) Good friends are happy for you when you score a better grade than them. They are not jealous.
5) Good friends encourage your ideas, even if it seems impractical to implement them.

The list can be endless; what you need to remember is your best friend will never laugh at you, will never exploit you and will never let you down. They accept you for what you are and for what you want to be.

As a parent, it's your responsibility to see who your kid's friends are and it is very important for you to know them personally. For as a parent, you cannot be with your kid everywhere, but friends will be.

It's a proven fact that friends decide our behavior, habits, mannerisms, and characteristics; if your kids are in good or bad friendship, it will reflect on them.

As parents, it's our responsibility to stop our kids from befriending the wrong person and at the same time, stop them from spoiling their friendship with good people.

In my experience, I have seen good friendships only in boys; they fight for some reason and the next moment you see them enjoying together. What I find more interesting is they will never say a bad thing about their friends to others even when they fight. They sort it out between themselves.

But it's not the same with girls. When they are in friendship, they behave as if there are no friends like them on this planet, but once they fight they start gossiping negatives of each other.

Girls may find my words a little harsh but it's true. Even girls will agree on this.

The best friendship would be between a girl and a boy. Yes, you heard me right!

Majority of parents, if not all, will raise their blood pressure when they find out that their daughter or son is befriending the opposite sex. But believe me, that's the safe bet any parent would want.

This is for you if you have a Son...

If your son's best friend is a boy, what are the chances that he will be joining any bad group or cultivating any bad habit like smoking or drinking or anything else for that matter? The chances are 90% unless you train your son to have a very strong willpower, as boys have this in their DNA; they are easily attracted to all bad things.

And read this now…

What if your son's best friend is a girl! Now, don't get angry and stop reading. Instead think, what are the chances that he will be joining any bad group or cultivating any bad habit like smoking or drinking or anything else for that matter? Only 10%, for boys always want to be in the good books of girls. Now don't get me wrong, it's a proven fact.

In the kind of irresponsible society we live in, girls don't feel secure. As parents and teachers, it's your responsibility to teach your son to respect girls and make them have a healthy friendship with them.

Stop… If you are a parent of a girl; think positively – what if your daughter gets a bodyguard when she is in/out of the school or a college? As a parent, is it practically possible for you to be with her each and every time? No, right? Then why not accept her healthy friendship with a boy in her class? Believe me, your daughter is in safe hands.

See, as kids, they don't have any filthy things going in their mind. It's we who plant that dirty thinking in their mind. We scold, sometimes even cane if our kid befriends the opposite sex.

Now kids will start thinking what wrong they did for parents being so harsh on them. Then they start looking at the boy or a girl in a different way, they start thinking of them, cultivate the habit of impressing each other, due to which starts an infatuation between them. And all things that parents don't want to happen, actually happen.

Tell me who was responsible for this? YOU. Yes, only you, my dear parents. You had that filthy thing in your mind that you transferred to your kid's brain. And then you again blame your kids for all your wrongdoings.

I actually started this book to teach kids how to build their character to be successful. But somewhere in the middle, I was convinced that it's not kids who need to build their character, for the actual problem is in the parent's mind, which has to be flushed out to make kids successful.

There is a popular American saying "Monkey See Monkey Do."

Do you agree that our kids are our blueprints? Then if you grow all filthy things in your mind about your child and do not trust them what will they become when they reach your age?
Answer: YOU

So, trust your kids, let them choose their friends. But as a parent, you need to keep an eye on your kid. For it's in our DNA.

CHAPTER 8
MANAGING TIME AND MONEY IS IMPORTANT

In the current world scenario, time is money. Any person who masters time management will be successful and there's no debate on this.

This is one area where a majority of kids fail, for we don't teach them time management.

Every person on this planet has only 24 hours at their disposal. But only 1% of the population on this planet is successful and 99% of the population lives a mediocre life giving all types of excuses.

My grandfather always told me, "To be successful in life, you need not be super intelligent; however, you need to be super at managing your time." He also said, "To master time management, and to leave the world behind, you need to start even before everyone is out of their beds. It means you need to wake up as early as 4.30 AM. And mind you, these timings are irrespective of a working day or a holiday."

It may sound harsh, but it works. But, as parents, we pamper our kids to an extent that they are habituated and start feeling that sleeping till late in the morning is their birthright. It is neither good for their health or academics nor for their career or life.

Before making your kid learn discipline, let them learn how to get up early in the morning by 4.30 AM, they will learn discipline by themselves.

Most parents ask me a question, "Should we make our kids learn the importance of time or the importance of money?" When I say let them learn both, the immediate reaction from parents is, "Sir! If money is lost we can earn it back, but if time is lost we cannot bring it back."

As a teacher, I totally disagree with the argument. I teach my students at AVR Coaching, both. Managing money is equally important like managing time. I totally agree that if time is lost you cannot get it back, but tell me, how can you earn back the money you lost?

For better understanding, let me explain you a story my grandfather told me about his life lessons.

My grandfather was a mathematics teacher himself, he was a master at managing time but was very bad at managing money. In the process of doing something great for the society and the community he lived in, he would donate a major chunk of his earnings to the people who would need it. Whenever my grandmother would oppose, he would always say next month he would again earn that money.

He asked me, "What do you think, what I said was right or wrong?"

I said, "Fair enough, yes, you would anyhow earn that money, right?" With a pause in his tone, he said, "WRONG, the money I would earn next month would be new money; the old money that I donated (lost) for people who exploited me would never come back to me."

With his experience, he taught me a very big lesson, which I teach my students at AVR Coaching.

"Time and money once lost will never come back."

Here I am not saying, don't help others. First, see if the person who is seeking your help deserves your time and money at the cost of your own family or not and then decide if you really want to help that person.

If you decided to help that person, keep in mind you cannot sacrifice beyond 1% of your current bank balance.

For example, if you have $100 (or whatever your currency is) in your account, you are entitled to help only $1 to the person who is seeking your help. If the person is okay with it, well and good, else your $1 stays with you, as each and every dollar you earn is the birthright of your wife and children; you cannot bypass them or ignore them to earn yourself a good name in the society.

Remember one thing, even if society says bad things about you - like you are not sensitive enough to understand others' problems and help them financially, it's okay. But if your wife and children curse you, it hurts badly.

Teach your kids to respect both time and money as we are not here to permanently settle down on the planet. We have very little time to make our lives meaningful, which is only possible if you're a master at managing both money and time.

Hope you understood what I wanted to explain…

CHAPTER 9

CAREER SHOULD BE BY CHOICE NOT BY CHANCE

Everyone on this planet will always have a choice – to choose or not to choose; either way, it's your choice.

Let us understand this with a situation: when you are traveling, do you get into any bus, train or flight and ask them to decide your destination or will you decide your destination first and then start your journey.

Unless you are an idiot to the core, you will decide your destination first.

This also applies to the career of your kid. However, career is a journey, not a destination. For your career doesn't end once you reach your destination. To be successful, you need to have a new destination.

But, unfortunately, the majority of kids who are in school or college are not clear about their career goals. They do not have the clarity of what they want to be.

This may be due to…

Parents have their own agenda

Parents have their own aspirations for their kids and don't encourage kids to have their own. Now, this is a big problem. As a parent, if you are not encouraging individuality in your kid you are destroying your kid's future with your own hands. As I said in chapter 3, don't be an enemy of your own kid.

As parents we should encourage our kids to design and take charge of their own life, we should be there if they need any help or guidance.

As parents, we always try to provide the best possible career opportunities for our kids. Absolutely nothing wrong in it. But, most of the time this is a reflex action which depends on the outer circumstances like:

- You want your kid to be an engineer because one of your colleague's kid is an engineer.
- You want your kid to be a doctor as your relative's kid is a doctor.

You are not worried about your kid's happiness; you are worried about satisfying your own ego in front of your colleagues and relatives. You want your kid to be a trophy to showcase your success.

Chill guys, let's have a break. If your kids are not happy in what they are doing and struggling in their life, will you be happy seeing them in that position at the time of your retirement? NO, you will repent and curse yourself for putting your kid in that position.

You may ask, don't we have any responsibility towards our own kids? Yes, you do have, but only to a certain extent. As a parent, you may be aware of your kid's strengths and weakness. So, keeping that in mind you can suggest them a career but you should not take decisions on their behalf.

You may also ask, kids who choose their career due to their parent's decision, are they not successful or happy? Yes, the majority of them are neither successful nor happy.

The problem with our so-called educated society is that success depends on the brand of a car a person drives, the house they live in or in being settled abroad (Anywhere in the world but not in their own country) etc.

But the actual meter for success is how happy they are professionally and personally. To the outside world, they may be living a dream life, but a closer look into the lives would get you the clarity that they are not satisfied with their own life. They are not actually living, they are just passing their time.

Today you are a parent, but you too came from the same age as your kid, where you had so many dreams and ideas in your head that you wanted to implement.

Put your hand on your heart and say to your kid that you are living your dream life; if you can say this to your kid then you are very lucky to have great parents who allowed you to live your dream. So, it's your turn as a parent now.

But most of the parents cannot do that, for your parents had the same kind of aspirations you have today for your kids.

No parents want their kids to be unsuccessful or unhappy in life. In this world, if there is someone who, from the bottom of their heart, wants kids to be super successful and happy are parents and teachers; everyone else will be jealous.

Let your kid choose their career by their choice and not yours.

By the way, why only kids, as a person you too have the full right to live your dream life. Today you are lucky; you can at least take your own decisions. Remember, it's never too late…

You might be thinking how someone like you could, with so many responsibilities, leave the cushy job and start building your dreams.

Come on… search Google, and you will get tons of stories on how people left their high paying jobs to start something new in their lives and are successful today.

I resigned from my job as a Software Engineer at Cognizant Technology Solutions which was paying me a seven-figure salary annually when my son was one year old. And today when I am writing this book, it's almost five years I left my job to live my dream.

Today, I can say I am happier and earning more than what my job would pay and most importantly, I am blessed to get an opportunity of shaping the young minds.

Every person will die one day; what matters the most is how you lived your life - on your terms or on the terms of others.

At the time you take your last breath, you should not repent that you could not do what you actually wanted and lived life like a puppet in that 9 to 5 job.

Now don't let this happen to your kids!

CHAPTER 10
SUPPORT FROM PARENTS

You open any book, listen to any speech from a successful person or any person who is being awarded for what they have achieved in their life. One thing will be common, almost everyone will thank their parents for supporting them.

Most of us would think these people are acting very modest, but they mean what they say. For, it's true that if there is no support from parents during their growing years, they would not be what they are today.

The first criterion for any parent is that their kids should excel in academics, then in life. Most of the time this is valid and acceptable. However, in current society, since both the parents should be working to have a decent lifestyle, there is no time left for parents to focus on their kid's academics.

I have already mentioned in chapters 1 and 2, the importance of mother and father in shaping their kid's future. It's mandatory for parents that they have full information regarding their kid's academic performance day in day out.

But the problem here is most parents who read the 3rd chapter of this book would argue with me that they have found a great teacher and paid a hefty fee to look after their kid's academics and now it's the duty of the teacher to see kids excel in academics.

But what you don't understand is your kid's success in academics and life is totally dependent on the teamwork of Student, Parent, and Teachers.

If any 'one' of them does not perform well, it will directly affect only the student.

Majority of the parents feel that their duty ends when they find a great teacher to look after their kid's academics. Actually, if you're sensible enough, you will get to know that your duty has actually started now.

Just sending your kids to good schools or good coaching classes would not be enough to improve their academics performance. It's very important for you, as a parent, to see that your ward is practicing what the teacher taught him/her.

During the months of February to April when the admissions are at peak at our institute "AVR Coaching", few parents try to put the whole responsibility of their ward's academics on our teachers for only one reason, they pay us a fee. However, we make it very clear that we charge a fee to add value to our student's life and academics.

For a kid to excel in academics, there are few parameters which need to be satisfied.

1) No doubt you need a great teacher.
2) Students and parents have to cooperate with teachers so the teachers can do their job.

3) Parents have to make sure that their kid attends classes regularly, for it's not the duty of teachers to come and pick up the kids from their place.

4) Parents have to make sure that kids are actually practicing what they have been taught in schools and their coaching classes. Teachers cannot control what a student does once they are out of the school or coaching class.

5) Most importantly, when teachers make your kid accountable for any incomplete work or their poor test performance, parents should not come running for the rescue of their kid. Instead, they should support the teachers for doing this.

6) For the sake of your kid's academics and life, you might want to sacrifice that late night party or a vacation of 5 days. Just do it, it's for the betterment of your own kid.

Even after doing all the above, if you feel that your kid is not improving in academics, sit and discuss the situation openly with the teacher. I am sure a parent and teacher together can come up with a great solution for improving the kid's performance.

Without doing any of the above, simply don't blame the teachers.

For any problems in their lives, any kid would first look up for parents' support, only then they will turn to their teachers.

When your kid turns to you for help, stand by them and never let them down. Try to build a relationship where your kid will blindly trust you.

For example, do you have any doubts in your mind for the food cooked by your mother? Do you test the food cooked by your mother? No, right?

The same way, your kid should have full faith in you; kids should never ever have a second thought to openly discuss what they are going through in life.

Whatever it may be, good or bad, they should have the confidence that you will stand by them.

You are successful as a parent if you come to know everything good or bad about your kid from your kid himself/herself. Not from a third person. Not even your wife or husband.

If you can build this kind of relationship with your kid, then no one can stop your kid from being successful, both academically and in life.

All The Very Best!

CHAPTER 11

DON'T COMPARE, JUST INSPIRE

Motivation is all it takes to bring the best out of any child, but what parents do is exactly the opposite; they keep comparing their kids with others.

Parents are in an illusion thinking that by comparing their kids to others they are telling kids to be inspired and motivated, which to some extent is correct.

But kids take it the other way round, they start degrading themselves in their own mind. They come to the conclusion that they cannot make their parents happy under any circumstances.

Let me give an example of my own student: How and why I stopped comparing my students.

In the initial days of AVR Coaching (my business name), there was a student by the name Satvik who was not so good at mathematics and would manage to score around 45% in the subject before he joined AVR Coaching. And there was this girl, Lakshmi who was already our student and would score around 95%. Both Satvik and Lakshmi were from the same class but different schools.

After three months of coaching with us, in the first test at school Satvik scored 56% in mathematics and Lakshmi scored 97%.

Now Satvik's mother came to our class. I thought that she was happy to see that her son had drastically improved in mathematics in a matter of just three months and had came to appreciate our efforts.

But to my surprise, she started yelling at her son for scoring only 56% when compared to Lakshmi who scored 97%, in front of all his classmates. This made him uncomfortable, however, he stayed silent.

She kept on pointing out how both she and her husband were working so hard to give him the best life possible, and even after making him study in the best school, the best coaching class, he was unable to perform as expected.

She would always compare her son with Lakshmi, and said both were practicing the same subject with the same teacher, but how come Lakshmi was able to score 97% but not her son.

Now, even I was convinced with what she said.

As time passed, it was time for the term examinations. I knew Satvik had improved a lot in mathematics and would perform better compared to his last test.

As expected, Satvik scored 65% in his term exams, which was commendable and Lakshmi scored 100%

which is a dream for any student and teacher. Yet again Satvik's mother came running to our office with the same old drama of yelling at her son and comparing his score to that of Lakshmi.

As usual, Satvik was feeling low even after scoring 65% which was good compared to his last performance, but his mother could not see this.

But this time I took a stand for my student and asked his mom to stop comparing him to other students. I tried to make her understand how her son had drastically improved in the last six months. However, she was not ready to hear me out and continued with her frustration.

She voiced how she was getting embarrassed in front of her colleagues when they discussed their kids' academic performance.

After a minute, there was such a silence in the class, even I was totally blank and couldn't understand what actually happened a minute ago, for I could not believe what I just heard.

While Satvik's mother was not ready to accept the fact that her son has actually improved in Mathematics, for she only wanted 100% in mathematics and nothing less than that.

Satvik suddenly got up from his place and said to his mother, "Mom, you are always comparing me to my friends who score above 90% in their examinations, but you never appreciate the fact that I am constantly improving."

To which his mother replied, "Yes I am not satisfied with your score. When your father and I are working so hard and providing you the same kind of facilities, maybe more (every parent thinks that) than what your friends are getting, is there anything wrong in expecting a better score?"

Satvik answered, "Mom, you are yourself a postgraduate and do you believe that you are earning a good salary?" She said, "Yes, for the hard work I have done in my academics and the commitment I show at my work, I am earning a seven-figure salary with a good designation."

Now the moment came when Satvik said, "Mom, here is my friend Arvind; his mother is equally qualified as you are and with the same experience, but how come her salary is two times more than yours and she has a more respectable designation?"

He continued, "When your parents and her parents both gave the same kind of facilities (maybe more for you) and education, in the same university, you both got the same kind of opportunities then why your salary is just half of her? I feel very embarrassed in front of Arvind to say that you're just a manager in your office and his mother is a vice-president."

Now Satvik's mother couldn't utter a word; she had no answer, she just left. And never came back to our office.

I was totally convinced with what Satvik said. It is so true if a parent compares their kids to others then kids will start comparing their parent to others. We cannot blame kids for this; they learn everything from their parents only.

If you sow an apple seed you should not expect a mango tree out of it.

He was my student, but he taught me a huge lesson in my life. From then, I stopped comparing any of my students. This time it was final examinations; I was sure Satvik would give his best, for the hard work he had put in. When results came, Satvik ended up scoring 92% in mathematics and Lakshmi scored 100%.

Again Satvik's mother came running to our office, but this time with a smile on her face, tears in her eyes and a box of sweets in her hand. She thanked me and my team of teachers for taking her son from meager 45% to 92%, which was a more than 100% increase in performance.

So, parents, if you want to bring out the best in your kid, don't compare them to others, let them be inspired. For this to happen, you as a parent have to motivate your kids to be inspired by giving them examples of successful people.

But never ever give the example of their friends or your friends' kids and most importantly, do not compare your kid to others.

If you believe that your kid is unique only then will you be able to handle them, else chances are they will become adamant and you will lose total control over them. This is so dangerous for the future of your kids.

So Don't Compare, Just Inspire!

CHAPTER 12
THE ADVICE OF EXPERTS IS CRITICAL

Most parents are in the illusion that they know everything about their kids and their chosen path of career; you are not an exception unless your parents trained you to develop your own individuality.

In chapter one and chapter four of this book, I discussed the importance of mother and grandparents and how they can influence the thought process of kids, which is so important.

But given the global opportunities and professional commitments, the concept of joint families is a luxury. Leave grandparents, even parents don't get quality time to spend with their own kids.

If we give a test to parents on how much they understand their own kids, 90% of parents will fail.

Not that parents don't want to spend time with kids. However, for providing a decent lifestyle and great future for their kids in this growing economy, it becomes very difficult for parents to sacrifice their high paying job, totally understandable.

Nevertheless, you cannot ignore your kid and their aspirations. Is there a solution for this? Yes of course! You do have a solution. The solution is in chapter three - Hire a great teacher. But the great teacher doesn't come for cheap or for free.

You need a teacher who can understand your kid, their strength and weakness. A teacher who is an intellectual but with a heart to understand kids.

When it comes to choosing a career option for the kid, parents play a vital role, so vital that they stampede the aspirations of the kid under their own aspirations.

In my career as a teacher, I have seen so many students choosing their career only because their parents wanted them to choose it. I discussed more on career in chapter nine.

There was this student of mine, (who doesn't want her name to be disclosed) who actually wanted to be a doctor, but her parents wanted her to be an engineer because getting admission into an engineering college and getting a job is much easier than getting admission into a medical college.

When my student was in class 10, her parents actually felt very proud that their daughter wanted to be a doctor. And the kid was very happy that her parents were supporting her.

However, parents are parents so they started doing their due diligence, on 'doctor' as a career for their daughter.

Since she was my student, they first spoke to me regarding doctor as a career for her.

I knew about her strengths and weaknesses and fully supported her to be a doctor. I even made them talk to parents of other kids who were actually practicing doctors with huge experience.

They even started discussing their kid's career option within the circle of their relatives and friends; some supported and some didn't.

When the kid passed her 10th class board examinations, she scored 10 GPA in sciences (as expected), but I was shocked when I came to know that she took Mathematics as her major.

When I called her parents, to know the reason for changing their decision, the two major reasons they gave me were totally unconvincing.

1) They said, becoming a doctor is very expensive.
2) The time it takes to become a doctor is too long; we even have to think about her marriage. If it

takes so long to just finish her graduation when will she be settling in life?

I asked them, who told them all this nonsense and said, if these were the issues, does no doctor have a great life and a career?

They tried to convince me telling their version of a story on how one of their relative's sons had failed in the entrance examination and could not become a doctor. He had to join a normal graduation which would lead him nowhere. They went on to tell me how his parents told them how difficult it was to be a doctor. So, they changed their mind and cleverly protected their daughter from failing in life.

As a parent yourself, do you think their daughter will be successful taking Mathematics as a major, do you think she will be able to at least score a decent grade? Even if she manages to score a good grade, do you think she will be able to build a successful career out of mathematics and will be happy throughout her life?

The chances are next to nothing.

The major blunder what her parents did was taking advice from people who are not qualified-doctors. Taking advice from people, who are failures themselves, is a sin in itself and implementing that advice to your kid's life is suicidal for both parents as well as kids.

If you really want to take an advice on a career for your kid, take it from the experts and people who are successful in that field not from the people who left halfway. This is because the people who are successful know the actual path which would lead your kid to their career goal.

People fail because they don't have fire or love or commitment to the profession they have chosen. So, by default, they fail. By taking advice from people who never traveled the path of success, you are laying a foundation for your kid to fail.

Please Don't Do that!

If someone in your family or friends failed to achieve their goal, it doesn't mean everyone with a similar goal will fail.

The important part of being successful in the game of life is 'GOAL'; however, even more important than a goal is the direction in which you are taking the ball (life). If you are going in the wrong direction, 100% chances are you will end up making a goal for the opposite team and you lose.

The only way you will get the correct direction for your kid's success is, take help of experts. By experts, I mean:

1) Teachers who would have trained so many of their students and helped them choose a career. For, if you want to be successful in any field you need a teacher. And there is no better person on this planet to give your kid the best advice of their life.
2) Experts in the specific field, which your kid wants to enter. For, they know the exact blueprint for success in that particular field.

Remember, if you are seeking advice from any other person who does not belong to any of the above two categories, then you're putting your kid's career, life, success, and happiness at a huge risk.

CHAPTER 13
TEACH HOW TO MAKE SALES

Our education is a system which is designed to test the memory of students and not the knowledge they gained during an academic session. This system is called the clerical system. In this system, one needs to just follow the orders and not use their brains.

Since we as parents are stuck in the system and will never be able to change it, it is better we encourage and train our kids to develop skills which are not part of the academic curriculum.

Every parent is desperate to see their kids outperform others kids in their class. But unfortunately, this does not happen and is not possible that every kid will outperform others.

However, with good teachers and teaching methodologies, it is possible to bring every student to the same level. Nonetheless, this cannot happen unless students and parents cooperate with teachers.

An interesting fact about academics is, in the process of scoring high grades, students do not focus on gaining knowledge about the concepts in the subjects. They are concerned about just vomiting the data they stored in their brain on to their answer sheets. This will not help them to be successful; this will only help them get a clerical job for the rest of their life.

Now, as a parent, do you really want your kids to settle down as a clerk for the rest of their life?

For any person on this planet to be successful, it's very important that he/she masters the concept of sales. Look around you in your family and friends, the most successful people are the ones who know how to sell.

Examinations for the students are nothing less than high pitch sales where they put all the information they know about the subject into their answer sheets.

If we assume that every student has answered all the questions in the question paper, even then there is a huge variation in the marks scored by the students. Some students score high grades, some average, a few will score low, and a couple of them will even fail even after attempting the complete paper.

Did you ever think why this variation?

This is only because the students who score high grades have mastered the concept of selling their answers for maximum marks, while the other students failed to do so.

Students who score high grades know how to present their answers, so the examiner will be impressed and compelled to give full marks. This is not intelligence by birth or God's gift; this is something every student can master with little practice, for which they need to first understand the concepts very clearly.

Any student can master the subject, whether it is Mathematics, Physics, Chemistry, Biology, Geography, Civics or any subject for that matter.

The best and the proven technique to master any subject is to teach what a student understands to their parents or friends. Here most of the students will shy away from explaining what they learned to their friends. But as parents, you can always support them by hearing their version of the concept.

Most parents, what they do is, they will simply tell - you read all the answers I will take an oral test. And they expect their kids to tell every single word written in the book for a particular answer. Having done so, they mostly put the blame of mugging up on teachers. During parent-teacher meetings they would say that teachers told us to make kids learn **by heart** every single question in the book.

Here a majority of the parents get it wrong, teachers are always saying to make your kids learn **by heart** and not **by hard**. But since you have a communication gap with the teacher, you make kids learn **by hard** the answers, making it HARD for kids.

There is a huge difference in learning something **By 'Hearting'** the answers and **By 'Harding'** the answers.

By 'Hearting' is to learn by heart, which means to put your heart into learning the subject, but what parents and a few inexperienced teachers make is they tell students to learn **by 'hard'** making the subject very hard for kids.

Instead of asking kids to tell the answers orally, it is always better to make them explain (teach) the concept they learned, and in the process, you also ask them to clear your doubts in that concept. This way a kid can learn fast and remember most of the concepts.

Till here it is clear - by making a kid teach, you can make academics more interesting at home. You as a parent will get a chance to know your own kid very closely and in the process, will develop a great relationship.

But when it comes to examinations, unfortunately, there is no concept of oral examinations to gauge a student's intelligence.

A student has to still put all the knowledge gained on the papers to prove his/her intelligence.

As I already told you, selling your answers to the examiner for the maximum marks is an art that every student has to master.

The most important part of academics is gaining knowledge; however, presenting your knowledge on answer sheets in a more appealing way is equally important. For this, handwriting plays a very important role, which has already been discussed in chapter five.

So, the next time your kid is preparing for a test or an exam, ask them to teach you what they have learned in that particular chapter or subject. And help them understand how to present the same on the answer sheet.

If every parent makes these small but very powerful changes in the way kids learn the concepts, very soon there will be no parent on this planet who would want their kids to outperform others. For, every kid will be outperforming themselves in every test and examination.

"If You Are Playing Your Game With The Intention Of Defeating Your Opponent, Then You Will Never Win The Game. You Will Only Win If You Are Playing To Win The Game And Not The Opponent."

CHAPTER 14

DON'T TRAIN YOUR KIDS TO BE PERFECT

"I Think It Is Possible For Ordinary People To Choose To Be Extraordinary."

– Elon Musk.

I love this quote by Elon Musk, the one who inspires me to think big even if you don't know how to reach the goal, but you are sure you will reach your goal one day.

As teachers and parents, we keep telling our students that Rome wasn't built in a day. And the beauty of this phrase is even we don't know the complete phrase. For, even we were told the same incomplete phrase, again and again, each time we got poor or average grades. Yes, it's true:

"Rome wasn't built in a day, but they were laying bricks every hour.
- John Heywood."

We forget to teach our kids to outperform themselves each hour, each day, each week, each month, and each year to reach their goal.

Every parent wants their kids to score 10 GPA in their academics. However, if the goal of getting 10 GPA is only the vision of parents, your kid can never score 10 GPA.

If only the captain of the team has the dream of winning the world cup, then that goal cannot be reached in a lifetime. Winning the world cup has to be the dream of the whole team, which makes the goal easy to achieve and attainable.

Here the team would be Student, Parent, and Teacher. Three of them should be having the same vision for a student to succeed.

To be successful and happy in life, teach your kids to focus on 'quality' and not on 'quantity' every single day.

Most teachers and parents only concentrate on completion of the syllabus ASAP but leave the fundamental rule of teaching.

The fundamental rule of teaching what I learned from my experience is, teach students so they understand the concepts so clearly that they should be able to explain those to anyone, even at 2 AM.

Giving the best is all about quality and not quantity.

It's the responsibility of the teachers to make sure that syllabus is completed on time. However, it's also the responsibility of the teachers to see that every student in the class is clear on the concepts.

However, even after the best efforts by the teachers, there are chances that students will not be able to remember all the concepts from all the chapters in all the subjects. Then what the teachers and parents should do?

Sit with the students, and chalk out all the chapters in which the student is very clear on the concepts. Clarify their doubts in the chapters they are weak, try to make them understand the concepts more clearly.

I know this is not something I discovered as a teacher; this is the age-old practice of teaching. But tell me how many teachers or parents follow this? Hardly one in a thousand.

Don't teach kids to be perfect, for no one, not even you and I with so many years of experience, is perfect. You will find so many spelling and grammatical errors in this book. But I tried to give my best.

For me, if this book can change the life of at least one student then I would feel the purpose of this book is fulfilled.

Focus on 'Quality' and not on 'Quantity'.

I cannot complete this book without mentioning my student Hina who is a perfect example to explain **Rome wasn't built in a day but every day.**

Hina joined AVR Coaching for her school academics. After about a month I could easily make out that she was not performing up to her efficiency, mainly in Mathematics and Physics. She is so hardworking that she would put hours practicing these two subjects, but even then she would not get the desired results.

As a teacher, we identified the problem that she would perform well when the test was only for one or two chapters. But she would down perform when the syllabus increased. This is a common problem for all students.

The reason why I am quoting Hina's example is she is different in many ways compared to other students. She is a student who had blind faith in her teachers and believed them to the core. She was ready to do whatever her teachers would say with respect to academics, even if it meant sacrificing a couple of chapters in the syllabus.

As I said previously, quality is more important than quantity.

We chalked out a plan for Hina listing the chapters in which she was absolutely clear in all the subjects. Then we gave her in-depth knowledge in all those chapters which she was already comfortable in.

Our main motto was - she should be able to answer any type of questions from those chapters and should not lose even 0.5 marks. And also, we made her understand other chapters that were not so clear to her. We trained her in skills of presenting the answers (discussed in Chapter 13) in such a way that she would cover all the key points needed so she doesn't lose marks.

This took a considerable amount of time for us as **Rome wasn't built in a day**. The most important fact is, her parents who shared her vision also supported us in implementing this methodology.

However, in the end, the results very fruitful and she clearly exceeded all our expectations; she is now pursuing her degree in Law.

In my career spanning 19 years as a teacher, I have never seen a student who would trust a teacher to an extent that the student's vision becomes the vision of the teachers.

I have taught hundreds of students who are far intelligent than Hina, but she stands out for the single reason that she accepts her negatives and is ready to learn what she doesn't know.

As parents and teachers, we should stop saying Rome wasn't built in a day and start saying, "To Build Rome You Need To Lay Bricks Every Single Hour."

AVR COACHING

HOW IT STARTED

In the year 2000, Vishweshwar Rau started AVR Coaching, just after graduation for the passion he has for teaching Mathematics on the advice of his friend Mr. Sunil. Mr. Rau was completely unaware that he was addicted to teaching the young minds of India.

After completing his masters, he joined Bank of America as a quality analyst and after that joined Cognizant. Mr. Rau considers the academic year 2006 – 2007 as the dark years in his teaching career as he had to be away from teaching for so many reasons.

In 2007, on the advice of his mentor who said, "If you want to have fulfillment in life you need to do what you are best at, YOU SHOULD TEACH," he again started teaching while working for Cognizant. A few years later in 2013, he left his job with a 7-digit salary and ventured full time into teaching. He has been shaping young minds since then.

Vision:

Each time we meet our students, at any point in time in our life, we should be proud of them and not feel sorry for them.

Mission:

At AVR we are committed to encourage and motivate our students to set huge goals in education and career and help them achieve those goals by providing them with the right mentoring under the most effective teachers. None of our students leaves our premises with a doubt in their mind.

Values (VISHU)

Verve: We instill enthusiasm in our students to learn new things daily, so they feel the same gusto of learning every single day.

Inspire: Every student of AVR is inspired and motivated to compete with self and improve their performance.

Security: Our staff is our nervous system and our students are the spine of our organization so their safety is of highest priority to us.

Happy Customers: Parents are our elite customers who entrust us to shape their wards' academics and career. So we take pride in exceeding their expectations in every aspect of our services.

Understanding: This is the core of all our services and values. The first and the most important part of our duty is to understand our students and their goals/strengths/weakness like no one else.

Teachers AT AVR

Teachers are the nervous system of AVR therefore, we make sure that every teacher is highly qualified with an excellent track record in teaching so that every student of AVR gets the same kind of exceptional quality education and inspiration which will help our students build a strong foundation for their golden future.

"We Do Whatever It Takes To Build The Career Of Our Students."

Ways To Contact Vishweshwar Rau:
www.facebook.com/avrcoaching
www.youtube.com/avrcoaching
www.avrcoaching.com
e-mail: avrcoaching.hyd@gmail.com
Call: +91-905-222-0303